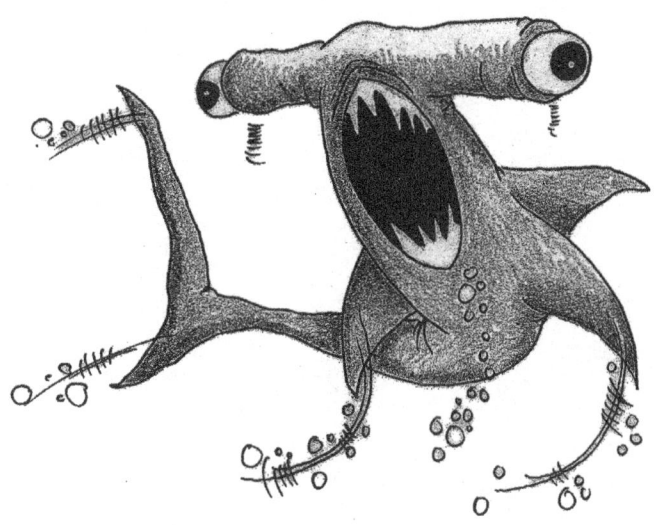

DRAW! DRAW! DRAW!
CARTOON ANIMALS

DRAW! DRAW! DRAW!
CARTOON ANIMALS
with Mark Kistler

Author Planet Press

Draw! Draw! Draw! series by Mark Kistler includes:
Monsters & Creatures
Cartoon Animals
Crazy Cartoons
Robots, Gadgets & Spaceships

Copyright © 2002, expanded and retitled edition Copyright © 2014 by Mark Kistler

Source: This work is an expanded edition of the book initially titled *Learn to Draw in 3D: Cartoon Critters*, published by Scholastic Inc. in 2002

Publication facilitated by Author Planet Press, 2014

Author Planet Press
7741 South Ash Court
Centennial, CO 80122
www.authorplanet.org

All rights reserved. In accordance with the U.S. Copyright Act of 1976, the scanning, uploading and electronic sharing of any part of this book without the permission of the author constitute unlawful piracy and theft of the author's intellectual property. If you would like to use material from the book (other than for critical or review purposes), prior written permission must be obtained by contacting the author at info@markkistler.com. Thank you for your support of the author's rights.

Author Planet® is a registered trademark of Jody Rein Interactive, Inc.

Additional material by Mark Kistler
www.MarkKistler.com

Designed by Carissa Swenson
Additional Design for Expanded Edition by Chuck Crouse
Cover illustration by Mark Kistler
Illustration inking by Chrysoula Artemis of Starlight Runner Entertainment

ISBN: 978-1-939990-04-4

To my student A.J. DeVol—his gifts of humor, creativity, and passion will continue to inspire everone who knew him for the rest of our lives.

WHAT'S INSIDE

A Message from Mark ix
Warm-Up 2
Bitsy Babbling Bugs 4
Meandering Mouse 8
Turble the Totally Tall Turtle 12
Multi-Mouthed Mackerel 16
Phanged Phred 20
Canyon Critters 24
Huge Hammerhead 29
Eerie Eels 33
Drooling Dino Dictator 38
Tearing T-rex 43
Cool Coral Colony 48
Conclusion 53
Cartooning Vocabulary Words 55
Mark Kistler Biography 58

A Message from Mark

The Power of Imagination

Hello, loyal reader!

Are you ready to draw some fantastically cool creative cartoon critters in 3-D? I sure am!

I think what I enjoy most about cartooning in 3-D is the ability to make *anything* I can dream up happen on that blank piece of paper. If I imagine a purple rhino with a helicopter engine strapped to its back hovering over my house while it sings lyrics from *The Sound of Music*, it can really happen on my paper—in three dimensions. Learning how to cartoon in 3-D gives you awesome Pencil Power! The possibilities for fun and adventure are limitless as long as you have your sketchbook!

I'm so anxious to get started! Let's get our fingers limbered up with the warm-up on the next page!

Dream it! Draw it! Do it!

MARK KISTLER

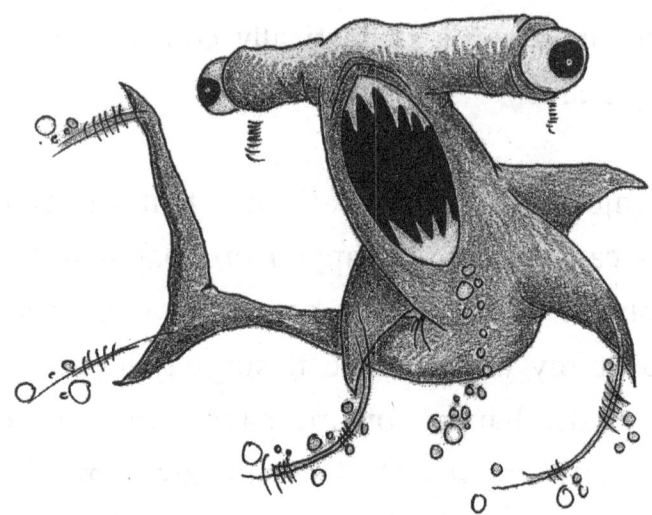

DRAW! DRAW! DRAW!
CARTOON ANIMALS

WHAT YOU NEED TO GET STARTED

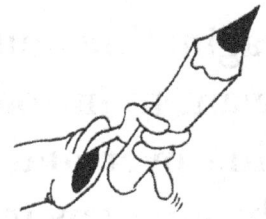 1. Pencil
2. Paper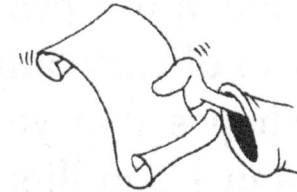

That's it! A sharp pencil and a blank sheet of paper are the only items you need to launch your brilliant imagination into the galaxy of cool cartooning in 3-D adventures!

BONUS SUPPLIES

To help you practice your important drawing skills every day, here is a list of bonus supplies you might want to collect over the weeks and months ahead:

1. Mechanical pencil   9mm hb lead (medium tip — good for blocking in sketchy lines)
2. Mechanical pencil   9mm b   lead (soft tip)
3. Mechanical pencil   9mm 2b lead (softer tip — good for shading)
4. Pack of 6 to 12 paper stumps (for blending your shading)
5. Several spiral bound blank sketchbooks in different sizes
6. A pack of colored pencils
7. A few fine and ultrafine black ink pens/markers
8. A special book bag to hold your supplies — your own "cartooning kit"

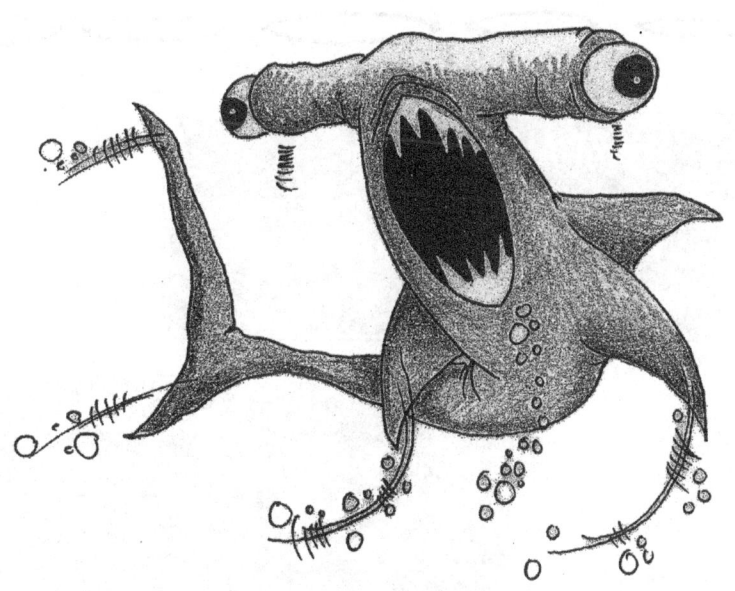

WARM UP

Before we launch our pencil power imagination shuttles into the creative world of cartooning in 3-D, I want to introduce two very important shapes that you will be using over and over again—probably about 1.5 million times—in the next few months. These two shapes are called a circle, and a foreshortened circle. Nearly every 3-D cartoon character and environment that you draw with me will be built up from these start-off shapes.

Keep your pencil lines loose and sketchy as you quickly draw two rows of circles like I've drawn here:

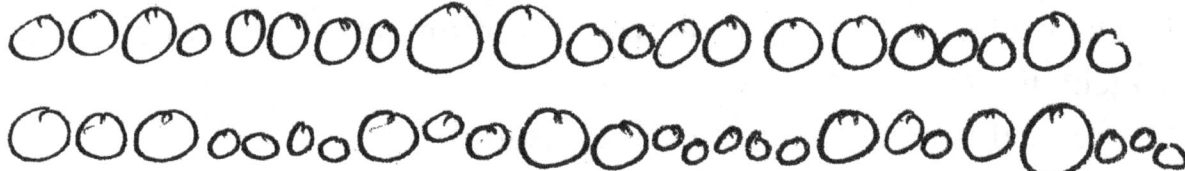

Now, let's practice drawing two rows of foreshortened circles. Start with two dots placed straight across from each other. Then, connect the dots with a curving line like I have shown here:

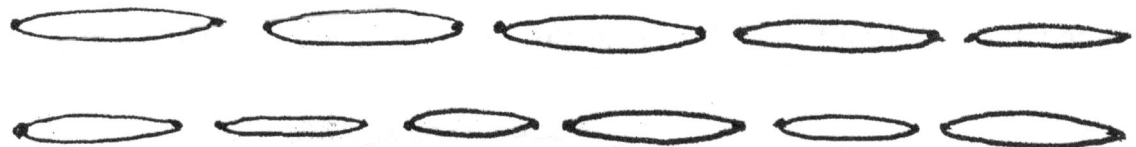

ART ALERT!
Whenever a word appears in bold, it is a very important cartooning vocabulary word. You can read a more detailed definition of these words in the back of this book.

ART ALERT!
During the cartooining in 3-D drawing lessons you will see this ART ALERT box pop up. In these boxes I'll help you understand an important point more clearly.

DRAW! DRAW! DRAW!

BITSY BABBLING BUGS

Bugs are extraordinarily cool critters to draw. Sometimes I'll sit on the grass in my backyard and watch itty-bitty bugs scampering around for over an hour! I'll put my cartooning journal in my lap and have a full-on wild bug drawing cartooning ART ATTACK! Let's draw!

1 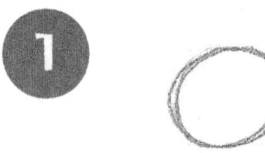 Begin this Bitsy Babbling Bug with a simple circle for the head just like you did on the warm-up page. Keep your pencil lines very loose, **sketchy**, and comfortable. It's okay to be messy; we will **clean up** any extra lines later.

2 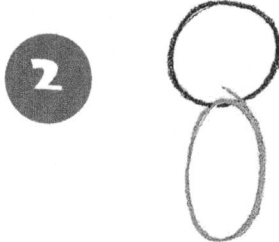 Now **block** in the bug's thorax with an oval. Remember to keep your lines messy, light, and sketchy.

3  Continue blocking in the bug's torso with another rough oval. Keep repeating to yourself "loose and sketchy, loose and sketchy, loose and …"

4

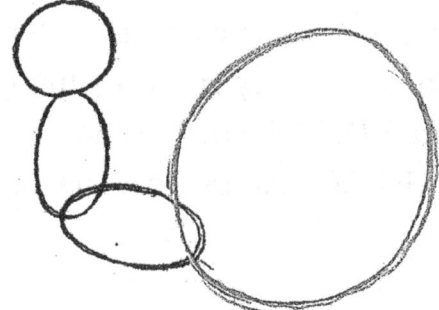

Lightly draw an enormous abdomen for this bug. Don't worry if it doesn't look scientifically correct. Since we are making up this bug as we go, we can rely on our **imaginations** to create a brand-new species of bug!

5

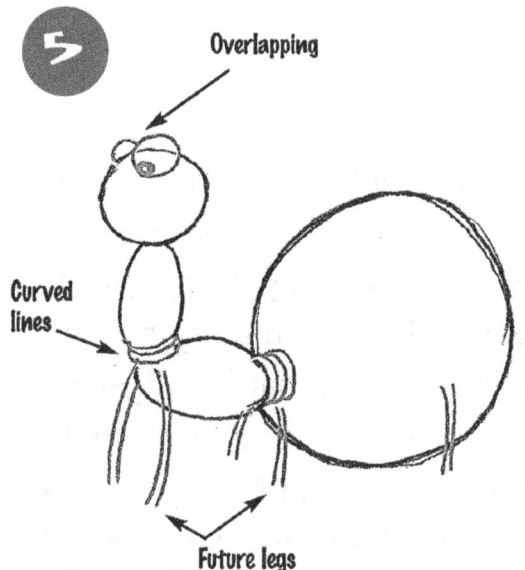

Overlapping
Curved lines
Future legs

Make one of the eyes really pop off the paper by drawing it in front of the other eye. This is called **overlapping**. Next, draw curving lines to connect each bug body section. Then, begin the lines for the legs.

ART ALERT!
Another way to make the front eye look closer to you is to draw it larger than the back eye. When you draw this way, you are using the cartooning vocabulary word size.

6

Guidelines

Let's work on the legs and feet. Under the bug, draw some quick angled **guidelines** to help you see where to place the legs and feet. When you draw along these lines, the front legs end up longer than the back legs. This helps the bug look three-dimensional. Now sketch in a few simple bent lines to begin the arms and block in circles for the hands.

7

Droop the antennae up and over the head and add a curving grin. **Contour** lines are curved lines that give your cartoon critters shape and the look that they are really living on your paper in 3-D. Make the toes that are closer to you LARGER than the toes that are farther away.

8

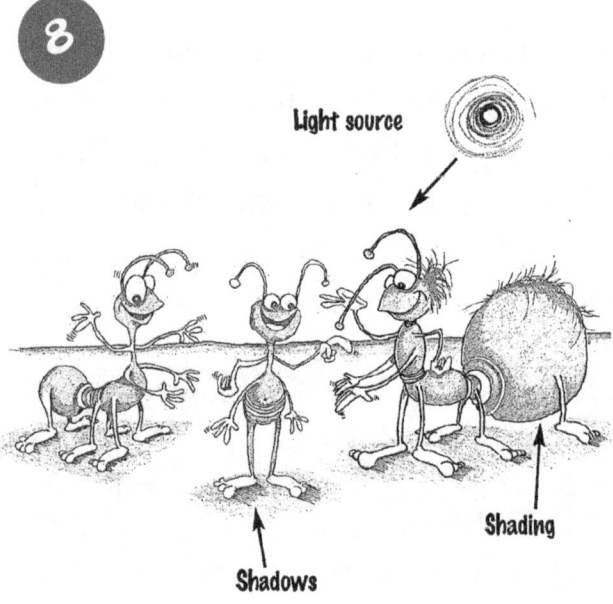

Final step! Final step! This is my *favorite* part! Let's add all kinds of cool extra **details** to our Bitsy Babbling Bug, like scraggly hair, dark cast **shadows** on the ground next to each foot, and the best part of all, **shading**! For this drawing let's imagine our **light source** is located in the upper right area of the cartoon scene. This means that all of our shadows and shading will fall on the side of our cartoon critter that faces *away* from the light. Use your finger to smoosh the shading into a **blended** tone from dark to light.

ART ALERT!
Next to your completed cartoon bug, create a few more Bitsy Babbling Buddies for your Boisterous Bellowing Burping Blue Bug!

ART ALERT!
To help separate objects in your cartoon scene you can draw some objects darker and some objects lighter. This creates contrast.

DRAW! DRAW! DRAW!

Meandering Mouse

I'm going to share a secret with you. Tomorrow during recess quietly, secretly, stroll over to the playground and very carefully look under the slide. You will find some VERY peculiar, VERY large paw prints that are ten times bigger than your own footprints. Do you want to know what kind of huge critter left those tracks? Draw the cartoon critter below and see in 3-D what the secret playground visitor looks like! Be careful, it moves superfast!

CARTOONING LESSON #2

Let's start with a **guideline** slanting up to the right. By building your moving cartoon character around this line, you can create the **optical illusion** that this Meandering Mouse is really racing toward you in 3-D! This little fellow is in a BIG hurry, so get out of the way!

Sketch in the shape of the nose, keeping your pencil lines loose. The action guideline you drew in step 1 should run right through the middle of the nose.

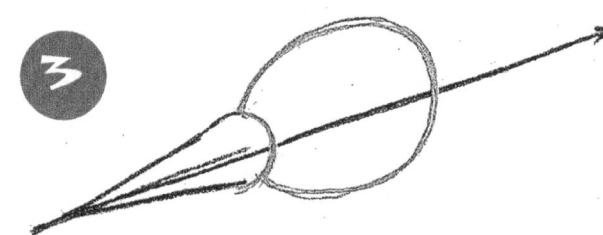

Block in the back of the head with a curved **contour** line. Now block in the big round body.

4

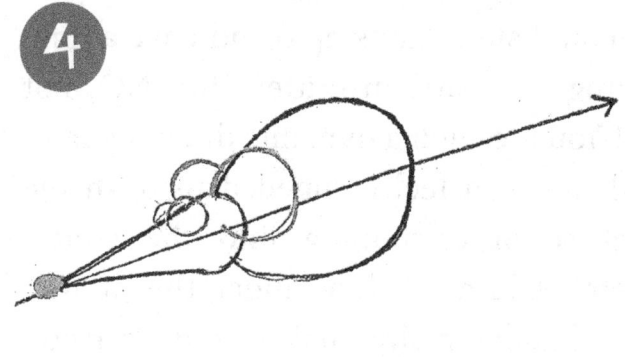

Add a bulbous black nose to the snout. This next step is cool! Make one of the eyes really pop off the paper toward you in 3-D by drawing it in front of the other eye. This is called **overlapping**. Then block in the round ears. Use overlapping again to push the back ear farther away and deeper into your picture. That back ear will also look farther away if you draw it smaller than the front ear.

5

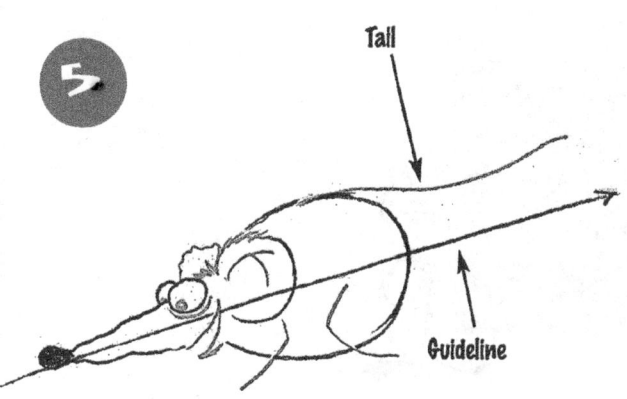

Tail
Guideline

Follow the long guideline from step 1 to draw the mouse's tail. Then draw the beginning lines for the running racing feet. Add **texture** by making the snout and ears a little bumpy and hairy. Texture is a great bonus **detail** art idea to add to all of your amazingly brilliant cartoon critters!

6

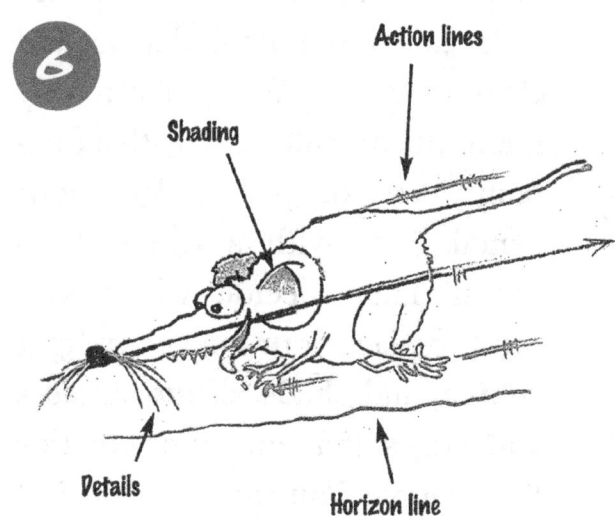

Action lines
Shading
Details
Horizon line

Let's work on layering on some neat bonus details. Draw in some whiskers, teeth, and a drooling, flapping tongue! I believe drool is a very important component in any professional 3-D cartoon critter! Don't you? Then draw a line below the mouse to show where the ground is. This is called a **horizon line**. Complete the running feet by drawing the feet that are farther away much smaller than the feet that are closer to you. Add lots of **action lines**. Look at your Meandering Mouse GO!

7

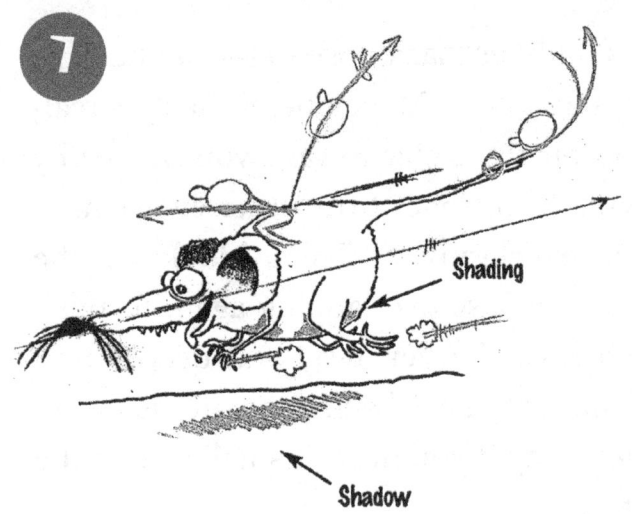

Shading

Shadow

You could stop after step 6 and have a fine-looking 3-D cartoon critter. But, NO, not you! You are such a dynamic drawing daredevil that you feel compelled to push the envelope of cartooning into the stratosphere! Add a **shadow** under the mouse. This shadow really makes your cartoon critter hover over the ground. You might even begin drawing some kids catching a ride on the mouse's back.

ART ALERT!

Action lines are fun swooping lines, and tiny little wiggling lines that help you create the illusion that your cartoon critter is moving, shaking, falling, jumping, running, etc.

8

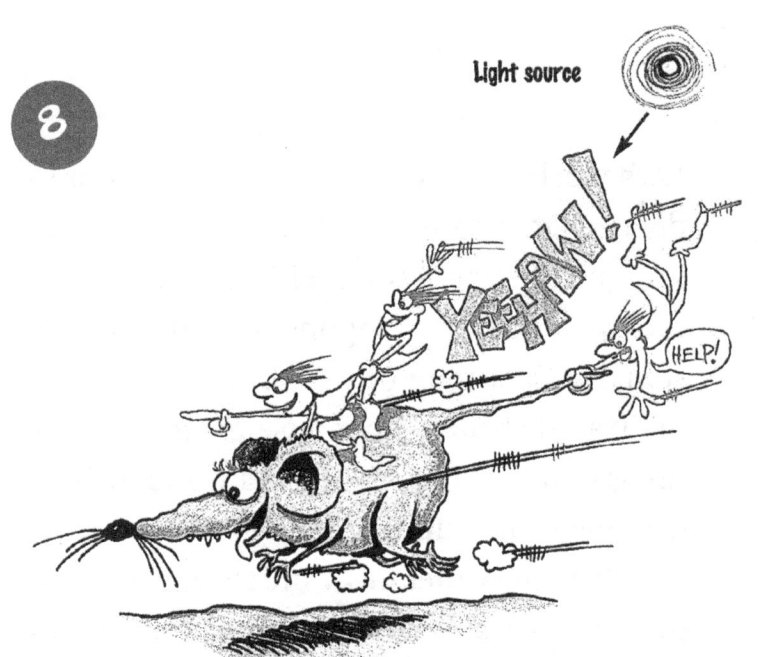

Light source

I absolutely love the last phase of every Dare to Draw in 3-D lesson. It is called the final details and **cleanup** phase. You can carefully ink in the outside lines with a fine-point pen, or just darken your pencil lines with a really sharp point. Then decide where you want to place your imaginary **light source**, and **shade** all the surfaces and edges that are opposite this light source. You can even add 3-D lettering for more extra bonus ideas!

DRAW! DRAW! DRAW!

TURBLE THE TOTALLY TALL TURTLE

My son Anthony has a pet turtle named Turble that has some very unique peculiarities. Turble has a long neck that can stretch almost to the ceiling and super tall legs that are long and skinny. These legs can extend so far out of his shell that Turble often steps right out of his fish tank. And get this—Turble wears sneakers! It's quite the funny sight. Turble clomping around in sneakers that are four sizes too big for him. Here, let me show you how to draw a family photo of Turble.

CARTOONING LESSON #3

Lightly, loosely **sketch** a round circle to **block** in the head.

Continue using light, loose, sketchy lines to block in the turtle's neck.

ART ALERT!
Remember, words in bold are explained at the back of the book.

3

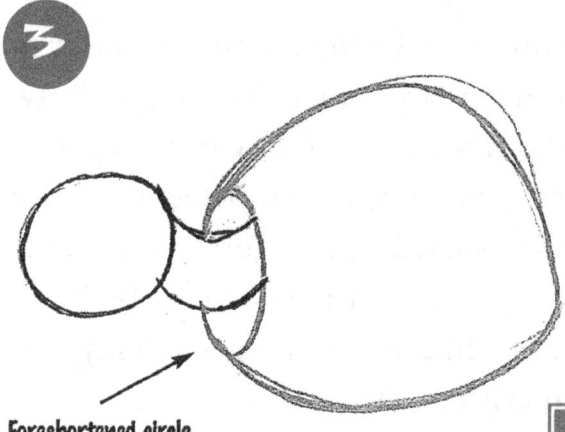

Foreshortened circle

Block in Turble's shell. You can make this shell any shape you desire—small, big, tall, smushed, or even a giant square! Have fun with this tall turtle cartoon—it's your own special creation! Then draw a **foreshortened** circle wrapping around the neck.

ART ALERT!
For a quick reminder of how to draw a foreshortened circle, turn back to the warm-up.

4

Sketch in Turble's beak, and add foreshortened circles at the bottom of the shell for his legs to stick out of.

ART ALERT!
Turn your imagination on to super flow! Once you've finished the lesson, you can invent your very own unique turtle by changing the shape of the head or feet, or by adding antennae, a different hairstyle, a hat, necklace, scarf, glasses, big chomping teeth, or whatever your imagination comes up with!

5

Contour lines

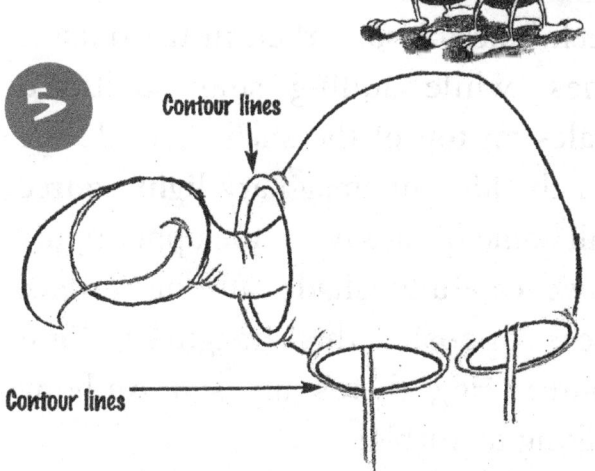

Contour lines

Draw **contour** lines around the neck and leg holes to form rims. Now add some **overlapping** wrinkles to the neck to give your turtle's skin that neat, lumpy, reptilian look. This is called **texture**. Draw a nice curving contour line for Turble's big grin.

6

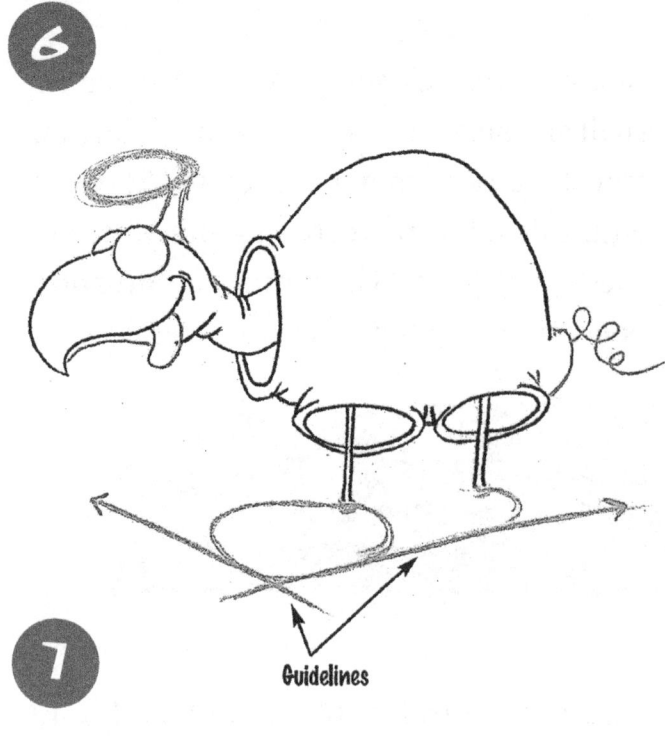

Guidelines

Be sure to make the eye that is closer to you much larger than the far eye. Draw **guidelines** to help block in the correct placement of the feet. Time to add a totally twisted tail to Turble the Turtle (say that five times really fast!). I always add drooling tongues to my cartoon critters. Do you?

7

We are really getting on a roll with neat little extra bonus **details** like the hair, the eyeball, and the drool. When you draw the back legs and feet, make them smaller and tuck them behind the closer, larger feet. Use your guidelines as a **reference** to **position** the back feet correctly.

8

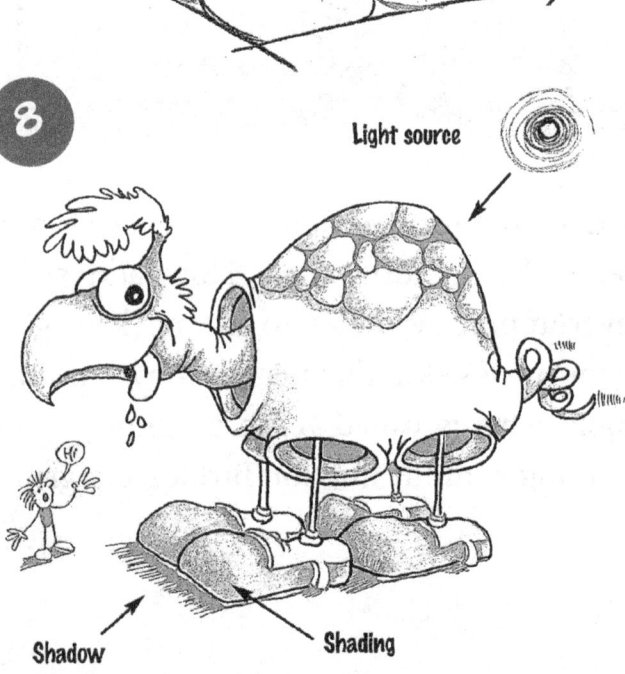

Light source

Shadow   Shading

Yahoo! Time for the final details and **cleanup**! Darken inside the leg and neck holes. Also darken in the outside lines, while adding some **textured** scales on top of the shell. Let's decide which side our imaginary **light source** will come from, say . . . the upper right? Now, carefully **shade** all the surface areas opposite this imaginary light source. Hey, there's my son Anthony talking to Turble!

DRAW! DRAW! DRAW!

MULTI-MOUTHED MACKEREL

Let's use our imaginations to turn our pencils into under-the-ocean exploration submarines! Prepare to dive! Dive! Dive! Keep your eyes peeled out the portholes—we are going to see some fantastic sea creatures. Oh! Look! There's one right down there!

1 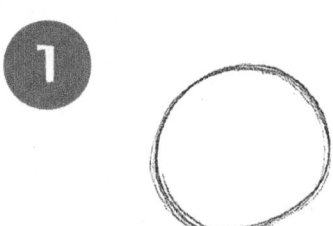 Start by **blocking** in a loose **sketchy** circle.

2 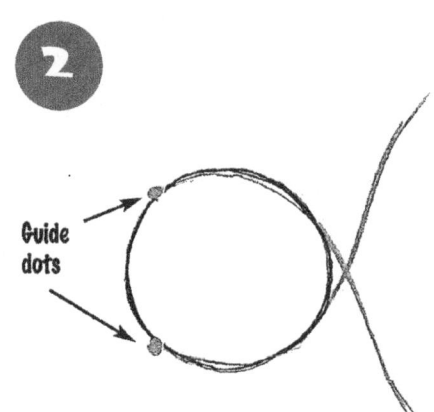 Now, extend the circle out to create the tail fin, also known as the caudal fin. I'm going to fan my lines out a lot to make this fin huge. Then draw two **guide dots** to position the mouth.

3 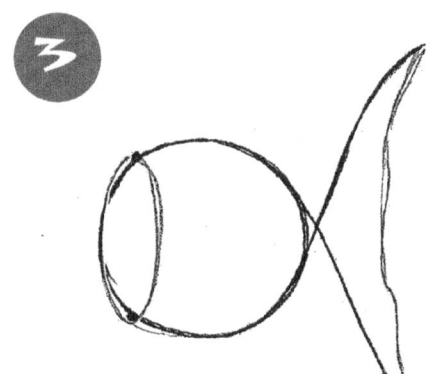 Using the guide dots, draw a nice **foreshortened** circle for the gaping mouth. Then draw a wiggly line to connect the back of the tail fin.

ART ALERT!
Remember, words in bold are explained at the back of the book.

4

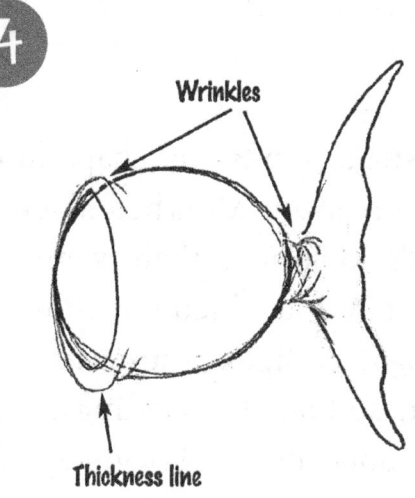

Draw curving **contour** lines around the mouth to show how thick the rim of the mouth is. I call these **thickness** lines. Notice that they don't go all the way around the mouth. Add a few extra curving wrinkles to make the fish look more 3-D! Let's add some curving contour wrinkles to the back tail, too. Looks good, doesn't it?

5

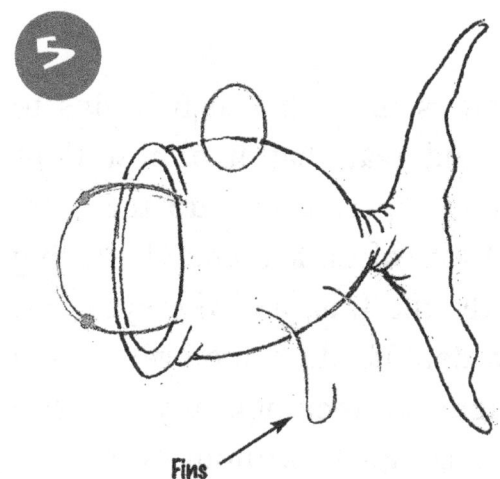

Block in the front eyeball. Draw the basic shape for the second gaping mouth and add two guide dots for the next foreshortened circle. Begin the lines for the side, or pectoral, fins.

6

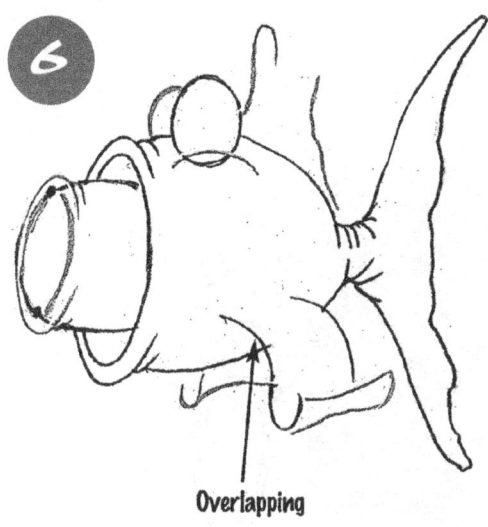

Now we really start cooking in 3-D with **overlapping**! Draw the back eyeball peeking out from behind the front eyeball. Then add the flopping top dorsal fin and the thickness lines to the second gaping mouth, along with curving contour wrinkles. Draw the peek-a-boo smaller back pectoral fin tucked under and behind the fish's body. Let's flip the tips of the pectoral fins up, like flying wings on a bird.

7

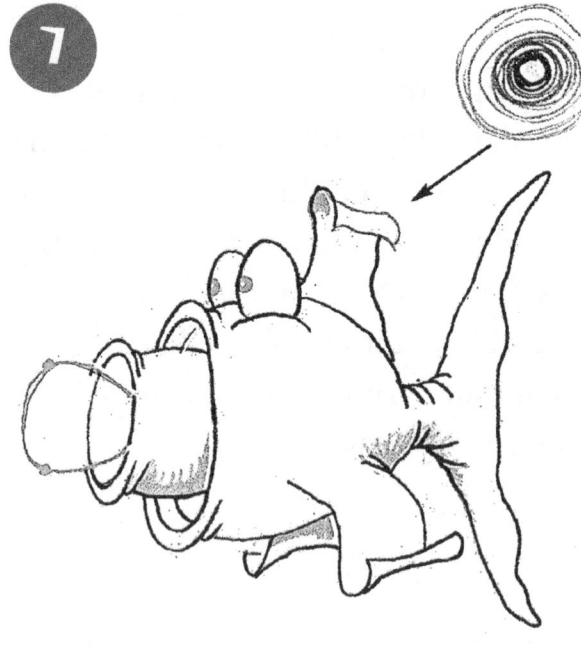

Light source

Darken in the small pupils and shape in the third mouth of the Multi-Mouthed Mackerel fantasy fish. It's looking rather weird and cool, isn't it? Determine which direction you want your imaginary **light source** to come from and begin adding the **shading** on the parts of the fish opposite that imaginary light source.

8

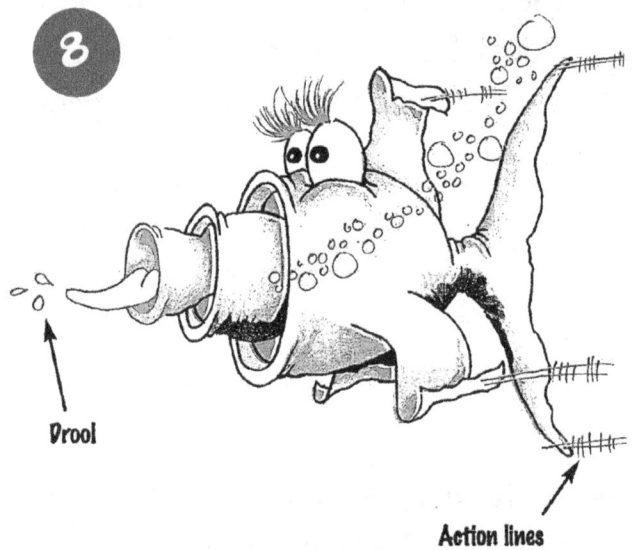

Drool

Action lines

Eureka! Watch as this fancy fish begins to look so 3-D and real that it almost flops around on your paper! **Clean up** the extra lines and add lots of dark **blended** shading under the body, the fins, and the eyes. For brilliant extra **details** add some eyelashes, a drooling tongue (remember, my cartoon critters are not complete without drool! Are yours?), and some more wrinkles around the eyes. Hey, how about some fast swimming action lines?

ART ALERT!

To make your cartoon critter's eyeballs look really round, shiny, slimy, and more realistic, leave a little white spot inside the dark pupil area. This little bit of remaining white area will give the illusion that light is reflecting off the shiny, slimy surface of the eye. Pretty cool!

DRAW! DRAW! DRAW!

PHANGED PHRED

We are learning to draw one 3-D cartoon critter at a time. Eventually, you'll be able to draw entire cartoon worlds with millions of different cartoon critters! Take a look at the cover of this book. It's a complicated picture and it would be difficult for me to teach you how to draw it in one lesson. However, when I separate the drawing into several smaller, less complicated lessons, you can learn how to draw this advanced 3-D cartoon scene one puzzle piece at a time!

1 Start Phanged Phred with a loose, relaxed, wobbly oval for his head.

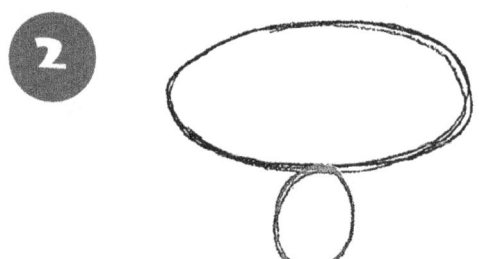

2 **Block** in his body with a smaller circle.

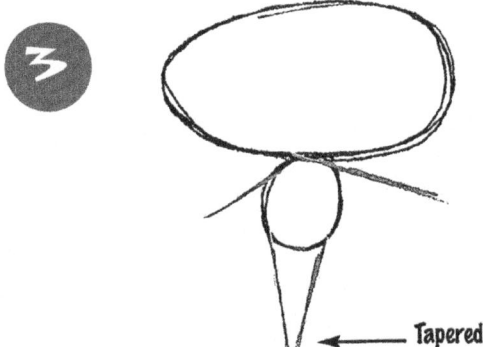

3 We want this fellow to be leaning on a treasure chest he has just dug up, so slightly tilt the standing leg of the body. Be sure to **taper** the leg so that it gets smaller at the ankle. Begin the arms with simple, quick lines.

← Tapered

4

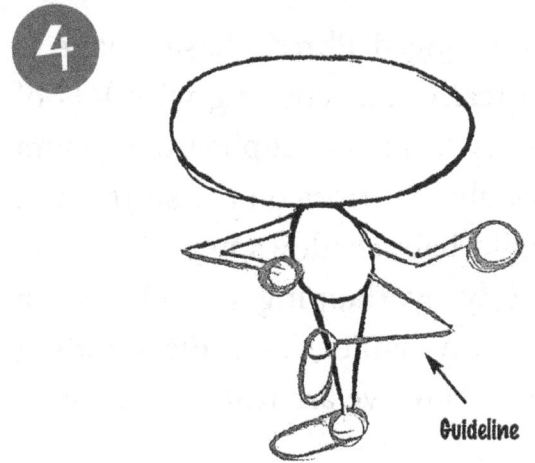

Guideline

Add **thickness** to the arms by tapering them smaller at the wrists. Sketch in the **guideline** for the other leg. We are going to droop the lifted foot down the side of the treasure chest, so block in the foot with a drooping oval. Now block in the other foot with an oval and both hands with circles.

5

Loosely shape the eyes with more circles. Draw your **guide dots** for the **foreshortened** square that will be the building block for the entire treasure chest. Go ahead and add the tilted shovel shape and some little circles for toes.

ART ALERT!
Check out lesson 9 for more info on how to draw a foreshortened square and a 3-D box.

6

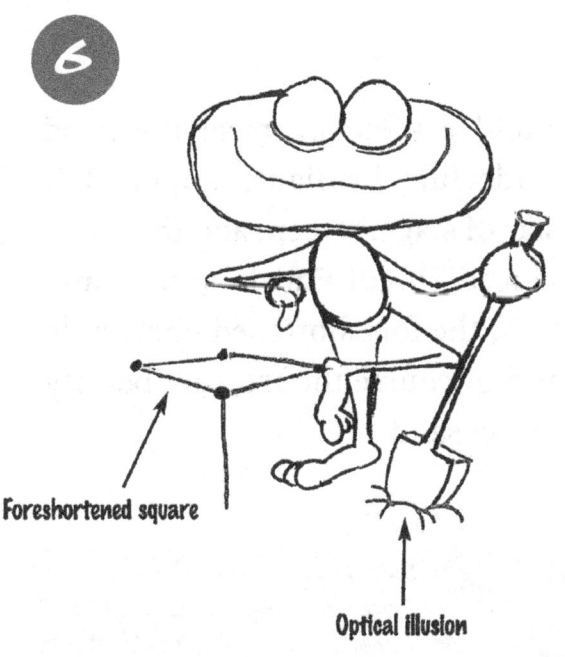

Foreshortened square

Optical illusion

Connect your guide dots to begin the treasure chest. Draw the nearest corner of the chest lower on the paper. Remember, things that are drawn lower and larger appear closer to your eye to make them POP off the page in 3-D! Curve a bunch of overlapping lines at the base of the shovel to create the **optical illusion** that it is mushed into the soft sand. Add curving **contour** wrinkles under the eyes to give Phanged Phred a fun expression. Contour lines under, around, and above eyes are wonderful **details** that add so much character and expression to your 3-D cartoon critter!

7  Okay, now that Phanged Phred's basic shape is formed, we can really start cooking with lots of special ingredients from our cupboard of extra spicy ideas. How about stripes on the shirt? You can add some wild hair, shadows near the shovel, and some puffy **overlapping** wrinkles for a more detailed, goofy smile. Continue building the treasure chest. Now we are really cooking!

8  More details, more extras, more ideas! Draw more hair flipping and flopping all over the place and some foreshortened cuffs on the shorts. Then finish up the structure of the treasure chest.

9  Ta-dum! Ladies and gentleman, meet my good friend, the wonderful, brilliant, super 3-D cartoon critter, star of stage, screen, and the cover of this book, Phanged Phred! Finish up by drawing the final details, the foreshortened circle hole in the ground, and of course the treasure bounty overflowing onto the sand.

↑ Foreshortened circle

Try drawing another Phanged cartoon critter named Phanged Phelicia and draw her hair curling all the way to the ground. Now draw a baby Phanged Phillip with only a couple of scrawny hairs on his bald baby head. There are so many variations you can try, practice, and create!

DRAW! DRAW! DRAW!

CANYON CRITTERS

A few days ago, I was walking along a canyon creek with a few friends of mine, all really quiet—too quiet! So I decided to practice my whistling and successfully annoyed my friends. As an even bigger bonus, I got the idea for this drawing—a line of quiet dinosaur hikers with one happy Whistling Willie enormously annoying everyone else! Sound effects, cartooning in 3-D, and idea-sparking all go together in a fun creative bundle.

1

Start with a quick line that angles up just a bit.

ART ALERT!
See how easy it is to draw cartoons in 3-D? Just one line here, then another, then another, and suddenly... eureka! 3-D!

2

Continue **blocking** in the direction and shape of the canyon with another line slanting down in the opposite direction. Draw each line—each zig and zag—longer than the last to create the **optical illusion** that your canyon is moving closer and closer to you.

3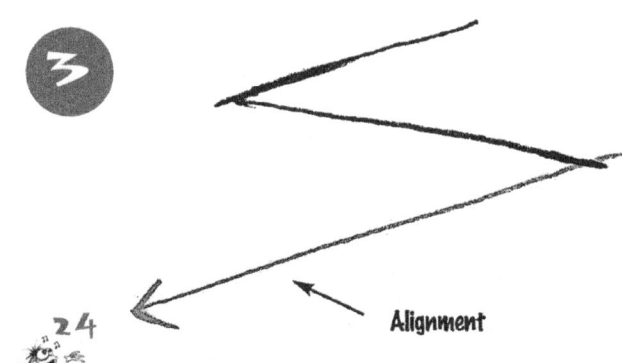

Alignment

Continue the path of the canyon with another line that turns another corner. It is important to keep your new lines lined up with the zigzags you have already drawn. This is called **alignment**.

4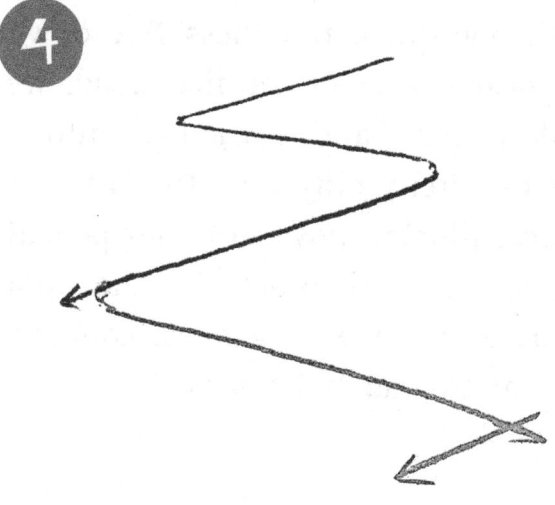

Let's turn one more corner. If you want you can keep going and make your canyon 1,000 turns and bends long! Just be sure to think about alignment as you draw.

5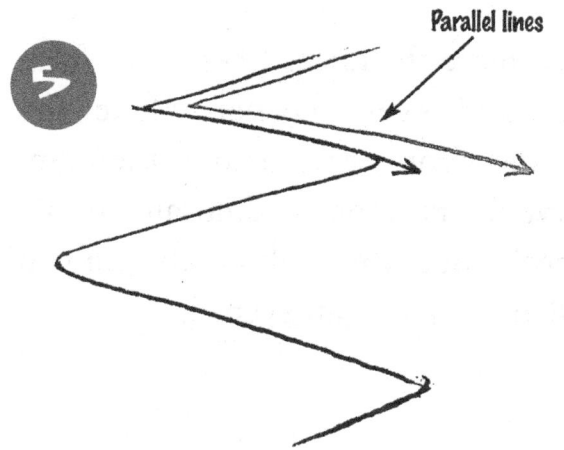

Parallel lines

Now start at the top of the zigzag canyon and draw parallel lines that line up with the lines you have already drawn. Notice how my canyon gets wider as it moves lower on the paper, closer to you?

6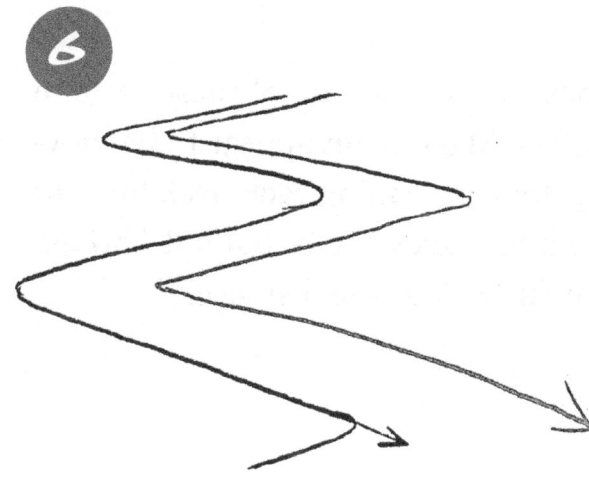

Draw the canyon getting wider, larger, and more **foreshortened** as you twist and turn lower on the page. This can be the beginning of a roadway, a river, or a long snake in the jungle!

7

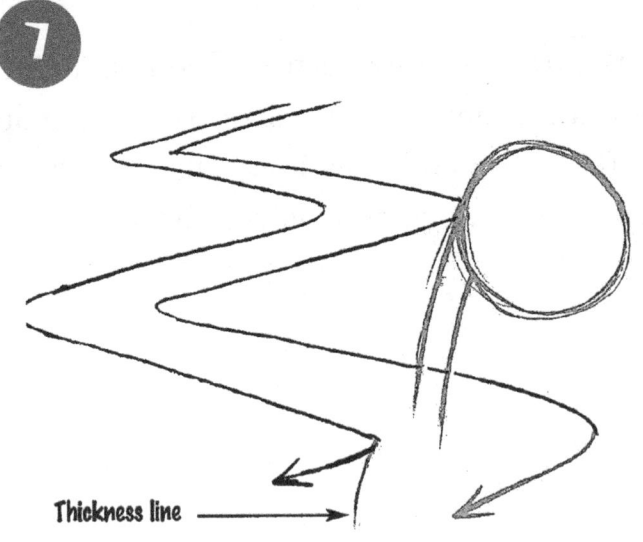

Thickness line

With one quick **thickness line** down the near corner of the first bend, we took a road and turned it into a canyon. Pretty nifty, eh? It's all in the **optical illusion** power of your pencil! Go ahead and block in the first dinosaur dude with a loose comfortable circle head and a neck.

8

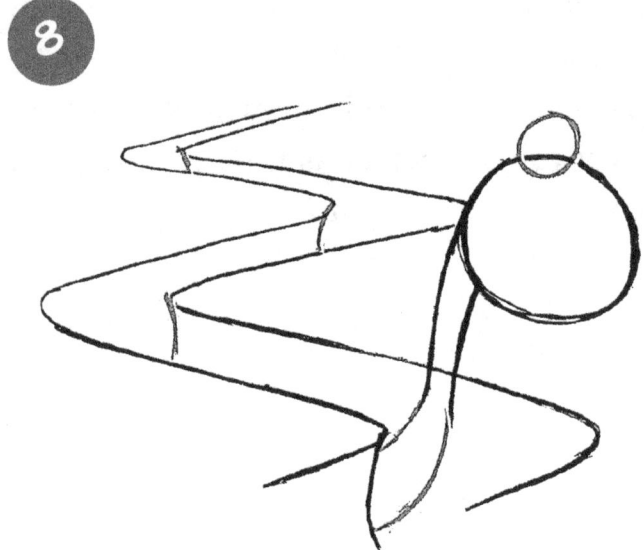

Draw more thickness lines down from each and every corner. Make the canyon drop way below the rim. Curve the neck of the dinosaur so that it peeks out from behind the canyon wall and draw in an eyeball.

9

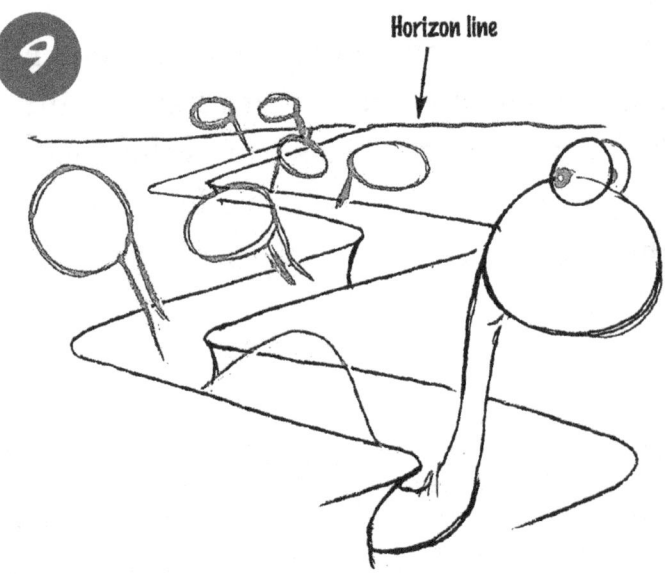

Horizon line

Block in a whole line of these cartoon critters. Make them appear to be moving along by leaning each neck forward just a bit. Draw the important **horizon line** far back in the distance.

10

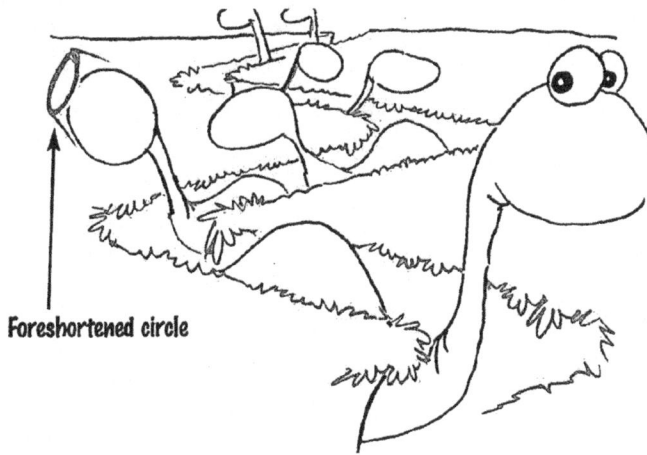

Foreshortened circle

Block in the Whistling Willie's mouth with a foreshortened circle. Then draw the drooping grass hanging over the lip of the canyon.

ART ALERT!

Practice drawing a few rows of drooping grass. Keep your lines loose, and have fun with this. I think of lots of W's in a row, some long, some short, some thick, some thin. Remember that variety of line is important! This is also a great exercise to warm up your pencil power engines before you begin drawing each day.

11

To really make the drooping grass tufts look 3-D, **darken in the area just under the grass**. This dark shadow will push the canyon wall back and pull the grass forward. Pop goes your drawing in 3-D! Add **overlapping** eyes to your row of critters.

12

Add lots of **shading**, **shadows**, and **details**, and **clean up** any wayward lines.

DRAW! DRAW! DRAW!

HUGE HAMMERHEAD

One of my favorite lifetime adventures (so far anyway!) has to be when I was scuba diving off the tiny remote island of Palmerston Atoll in the South Pacific Ocean. Less than 100 people live on Palmerstone, and they only get a few sailboat visitors each year. When I went scuba diving there were nearly 100 sharks swimming far below me. AHHH! Do you want to draw one?

CARTOONING LESSON #7

1 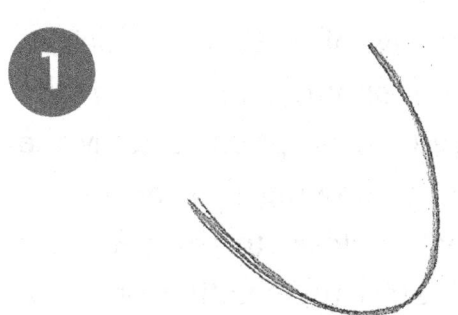 Let's start this drawing of our ferocious fanged friend with a quick, swooping U-shaped line, keeping it loose and **sketchy**.

2 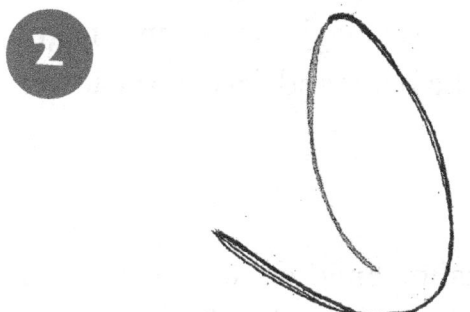 **Block** in the snout of this beast with another quick, swooping line.

3 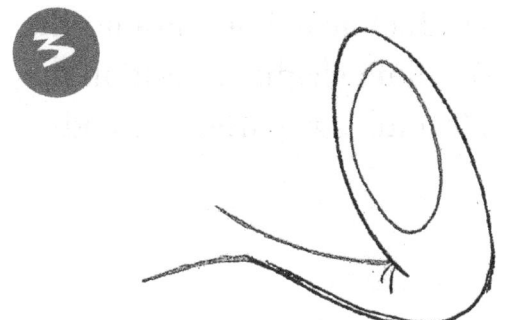 Draw a line above the bottom edge of the swooping line to form the top of the tail. Bend the tail back by **tapering** the lines so they get smaller and smaller as the tail moves away from you in the picture. Add a couple of **overlapping** wrinkles at the bend in the body. Roughly sketch in a foreshortened circle for the shark's mouth. Begin fanning out the end of the tail for the caudal fin.

4

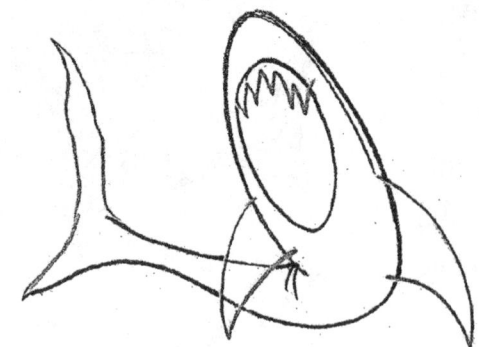

Draw in the top row of teeth with a jagged sawtooth line. Block in where the side pectoral fins will be. Finish the tail by stretching the top of its caudal fin much longer than the bottom. This long caudal tail is the shark's hunting tool. The shark snaps the long end of its tail around to strike its prey. WHAP!

5

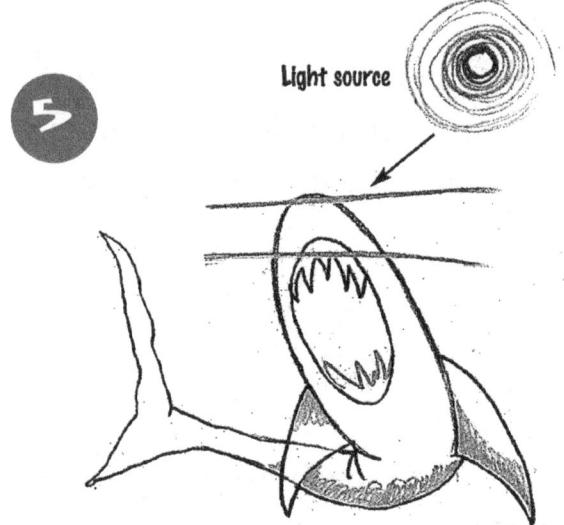

Draw the bottom row of teeth, and block in the hammer skull snout. This is a really funky-shaped head. It's so prehistoric! Make sure to use **size** by drawing the end of the hammer skull that is closer to you LARGER than the far end. Start the **shading** phase of the cartoon by determining where you want to **position** your imaginary **light source**. I'll put mine in the top right area, and begin shading under the body and fins on the lower left side.

6

Add a nice **foreshortened** circle to the closer end of the Huge Hammerhead's skull, and bulb out the little rounded line for the top of the snout. Draw **thickness** lines around the mouth. Then continue shading. Position the back dorsal fin leaning away from the body.

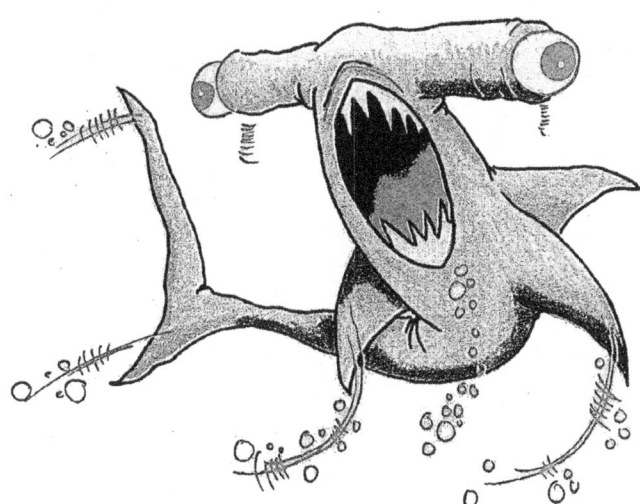

Ohhh, this Huge Hammerhead is getting so scary—but we are almost done. Just watch your fingers near this bad boy's teeth. CHOMP! **Clean up** any extra lines and **blend** the shading. Draw the eyeballs bulging while adding the cool overlapping contour wrinkles around the eyeballs. Of course the **action lines** rule this drawing so don't forget to add them.

ART ALERT!
Action lines rock your 3-D cartoon creation right off the paper!

ART ALERT!
One of the most POWERFUL 3-D cartooning vocabulary words to learn is shading. Shading is when you darken in the parts of your critter that face away from an imaginary light source. As you draw a cartoon critter, it is very important to decide where you want to place your imaginary light source (a sun, moon, shooting star for outside, or a lightbulb, lamp, reflection if your object is drawn inside a space). Then consistently darken in ALL the areas opposite the light source.

DRAW! DRAW! DRAW!

EERIE EELS

Would you like to learn how to draw some more of the cool cartoon critters from the cover of this book? How about those finicky fanged fellows bubbling under the island?

1

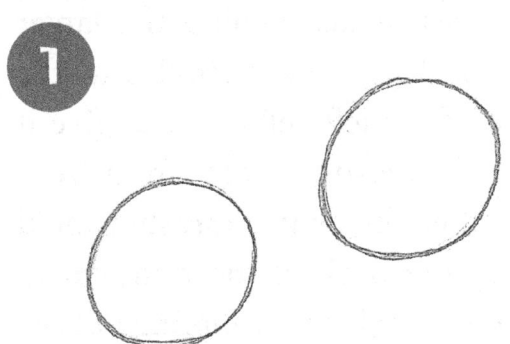

Every cartoon you will ever draw begins with a simple line—either curving or straight. For these two eel pals, turn two simple curved lines into circles to **block** in the shape of the eels' heads. Now look at the cover of this book. In just a few minutes you are going to transform those two flat circles into two really weird-looking 3-D Eerie Eels!

2

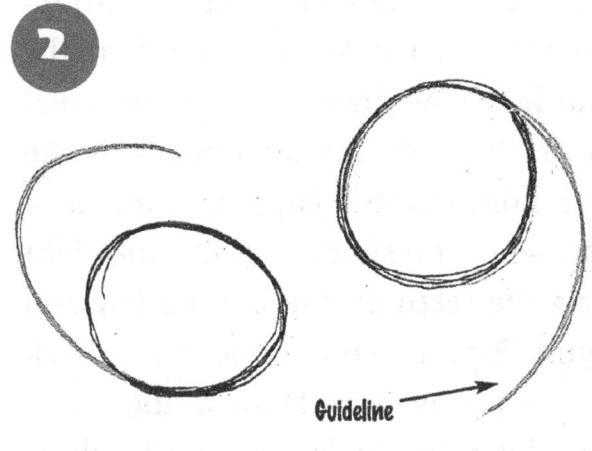

Guideline

Swoop a curved line off each head to create a **guideline** for the eels' bodies.

ART ALERT!
Later on, I want you to study how I have drawn the other details on the cover and practice drawing them in your sketchbook! When you are ready, take all your practice sketches and put them together to create your own special brilliant cartoon scene!

Blocking is important in this drawing. Block in each eel's front eye, the **position** of their gaping jaws, and the **thickness** of their necks. I'm going to give the eel on the left a closed mouth and the eel on the right an open mouth.

Draw in some jagged teeth and the smaller peek-a-boo eyes tucked behind the larger front eyeballs. Add a few wrinkles to the inside curve of the left eel's neck to give it the illusion of twisting away from you. Using **guide dots**, block in a **foreshortened** circle around the neck of the right eel to create the hole it will be swimming out of.

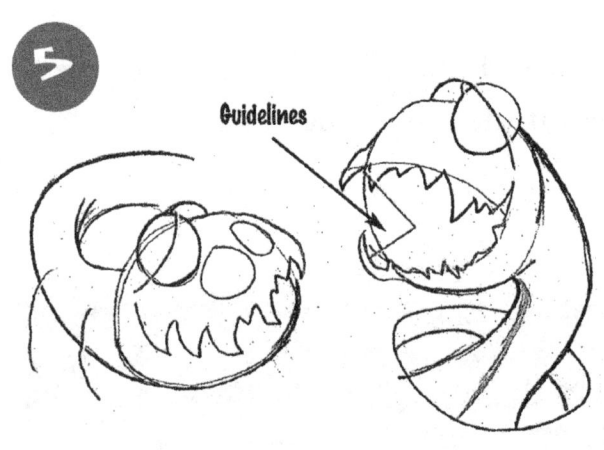

Draw curved **contour** lines for the drooping eyelids. On the left eel, block in the pectoral fin. Now draw two foreshortened circles on its snout for the nostrils. Make sure the front circle is larger and the back circle is more foreshortened. On the right eel draw the teeth on the bottom jaw and two guidelines to show where the back edge of its jaw will be. Draw a line on its chest to show the **thickness**. This is where the scales will be. Also draw in the thickness line on the inside edge of the hole it is swimming out of.

6

Whew, now we are really getting into **detail** mania! On the left eel, draw a jagged line along the eel's back for the detailed fin. Notice how it follows the top edge of the eel's back all the way across its body? Draw curving contour wrinkles, thickness lines inside the nostril holes, and darken in the shadows under the overhanging teeth. GRRRRrrrrrr, looking pretty neat and 3-D, eh? On the right eel, add the far rows of teeth in the gaping mouth along the guidelines we drew in step 5. Block in the direction of the scales on its chest. Shape the neck a little more, and darken in the menacing hole it is swimming out of.

7

Draw some bubbles burping up to the surface, **clean up** any extra lines, and add lots of wonderful dark **shading** to these Exuberant Eels of the ocean depths! By adding foreshortened semicircles above the eels, and around the eye like I did on the front cover, you create the delightful optical illusion of water rippling overhead! Cartooning in 3-D is like magic I tell you!

ART ALERT!
Remember, YOU can learn how to draw anything in 3-D—no matter how difficult it looks—because every drawing begins with one simple line that builds slowly from there. If you follow me in each cartooning lesson and learn the cartoon vocabulary words at the back of this book, you will be drawing professional looking 3-D cartoons before you put your pencil down!

DRAW! DRAW! DRAW!

DROOLING DINO DICTATOR

Let's buckle into our pencil rockets and time warp back a few bazillion years to Dinosaur Valley where we will request a meeting with the royal queen of Dinosaur Valley. The queen is a very special pterodactyl. Not only is she the youngest ruling queen Dinosaur Valley has ever had, but she is also the first queen to ever declare that all school recesses would be two hours long.

1 We will start this cool cartooning-in-3-D time traveling-dinosaur adventure by drawing a simple 3-D box. Start with two **guide dots** drawn horizontally far apart.

2 Now put your finger in between the two dots you have just drawn and draw a dot above your finger and a dot below your finger, just like I have done here.

3  Connect the dots to create a nice **foreshortened** square.

ART ALERT!

Draw 27 foreshortened squares before you continue with this lesson. Practice drawing foreshortened squares and 3-D boxes every day! The more practice, the more 3-D your cartoons will be!

4

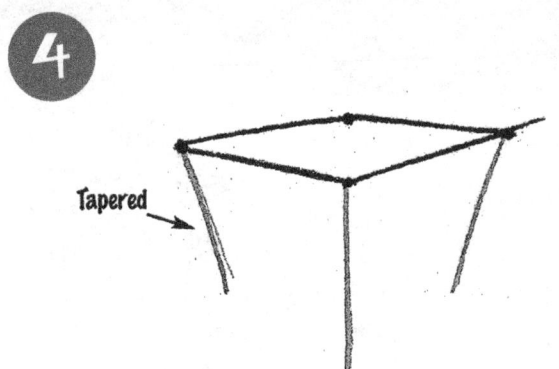

Tapered

Draw a vertical line down from the bottom middle dot to the center of the box. Slant the outside lines of the box a bit as you draw them to give your chair a nice **tapered** look.

5

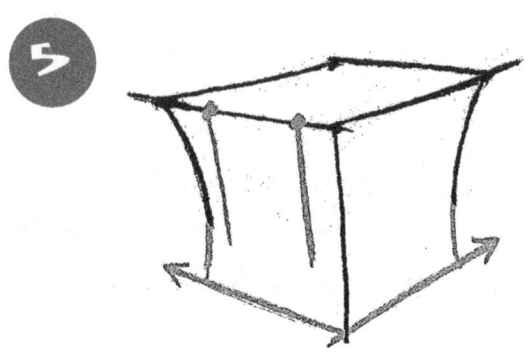

Connect the bottom of the box as you continue to curve out the sides a teeny bit. These little flared curves will give your cartoon a nice feeling of **style**. Draw two guide dots on the front edge of your original foreshortened square, as I've done. These dots will guide your lines as you draw the seat of the royal throne as well as the Dinosaur Queen's legs and feet. Draw two vertical lines down from these guide dots. Use the side of your paper as a visual **reference** for these two straight vertical lines.

6

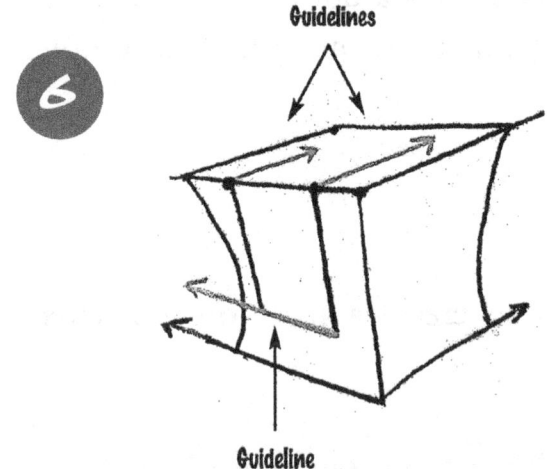

Guidelines

Guideline

Using more **guidelines**, draw the seat of the throne and begin drawing the armrests.

ART ALERT!
Remember, words in bold are explained at the back of the book.

7

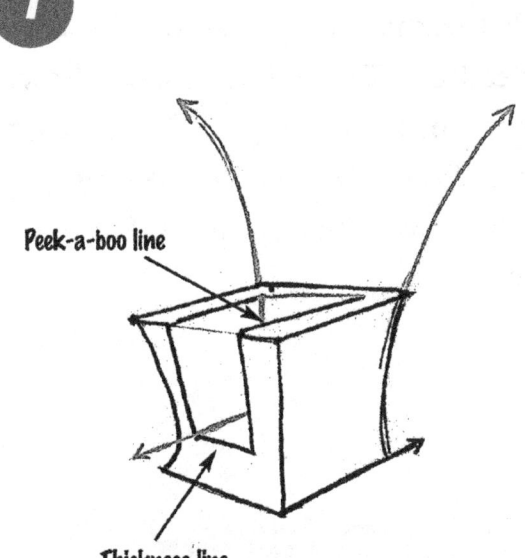

Flare out the back lines to create a really neat-looking backrest. Complete the seat by adding the bottom **thickness** line and the tiny peek-a-boo thickness line to the backrest.

8

There are many guidelines to draw in this lesson. They will help keep your throne looking solidly 3-D. Without guidelines, drawings often look distorted, like they are melting off your paper. Shoot the guideline between the two flared back lines in a long swift movement to form the top of the backrest. Remember to follow the lines you have already drawn—use them as a **reference**! Draw the thickness of the backrest, and carve out the fancy scoop for the queen's headrest. More guidelines create the thickness for the top of the backrest.

Finish the thickness lines on the back and headrest. Ta-dum! You have drawn a very nifty-looking 3-D cartoon throne. Now it's time to comfortably seat the royal matriarch of Dinosaur Valley.

ART ALERT!
Go ahead and erase any extra lines now. I usually wait until the last step in the lesson to clean up extra lines, but as we get into more advanced cartoons we will sometimes need to clean up as we move along in order to see clearly what we are drawing. If we don't, the drawing will get confusing. "Yikes! I can't tell where the neck ends and the chair begins! What have I drawn? HELP!"

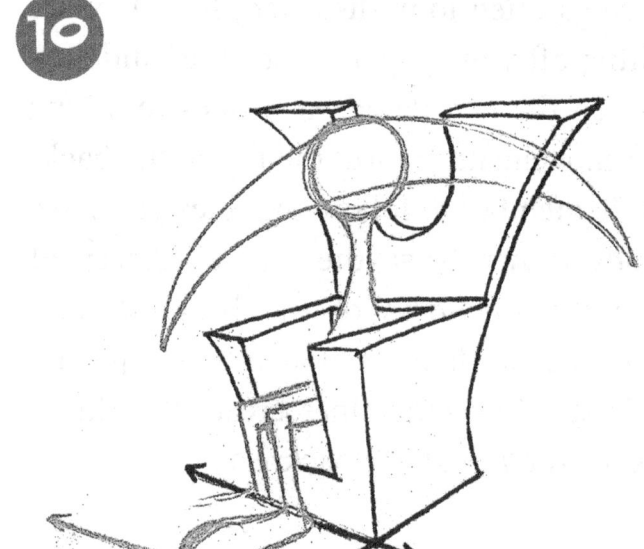

Block in the queen's head, beak, and neck. Draw these lines right over the lines you have drawn for the throne. Block in the legs bending over the edge of the seat. Line the leg lines up with the chair. Notice how I've tapered the legs a bit—tapered arms, legs, and necks look more pleasing to the eye, more professional, and more **three-dimensional**. Line the bottom of the front foot up with the guideline you used to draw the bottom of the throne.

11

Foreshortened circle

Block in her royal crown. Use a foreshortened circle for the top and contour lines for the band that holds the crown on her head. Now **sketch** in her overlapping eyeballs and the wing that is closest to you drooping over the front armrest. Once again, be sure to follow the angle of the lines you have already drawn for the chair. Go ahead and do a partial clean up of the extra lines behind the front wing and legs. Block in the back waving wing, and the back peek-a-boo foot.

12

Light source

Cast shadow

Eureka! We made it to the final clean up and **detail** stage! Whew, that was the most difficult lesson so far! You did a great job! Way to draw, you cartooning mega-achiever! Add bonus details all over your cartoon. **Shade** inside the royal crown, the wings, beak, body, and toes. **Shade** every nook and cranny on the opposite side of our imaginary **light source**, and add a cast **shadow** on the ground beneath her feet. For the final perfect touch, add drool to our Drooling Dino Dictator!

DRAW! DRAW! DRAW!

TEARING T-REX

After mingling with the royal Drooling Dino Dictator, let's take a hike across the castle's courtyard. We need to investigate a roaring, ripping, slobbering, gnashing sound coming from just around the corner. As we turn the corner we see the ghastly source of this super-loud sound—the queen's pet T-rex tearing up all the kids' homework! YIKES!

CARTOONING LESSON #10

1

Begin the Tearing T-rex with a simple, **sketchy** circle for his head.

2

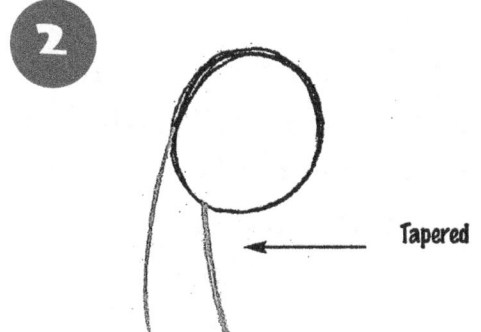

← Tapered

Block in the neck with slightly **tapered** lines.

3

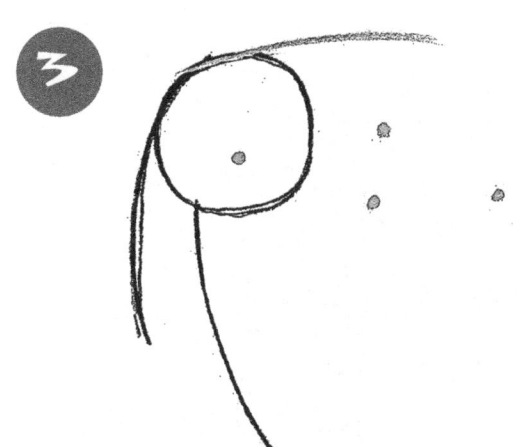

Draw a line for the top of his snout. To create the open 3-D mouth, let's use **guide dots** to build a **foreshortened** square (just like we did in steps 1 through 3 of the Drooling Dino Dictator lesson). Just about any object you want to draw in 3-D can be molded from a foreshortened square or circle!

43

4

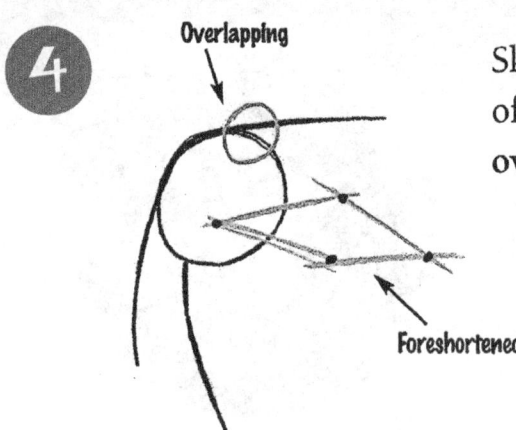
Overlapping
Foreshortened square

Sketch in the foreshortened square to create the roof of the open mouth. Add the front eyeball. It should **overlap** the top line of the head.

5

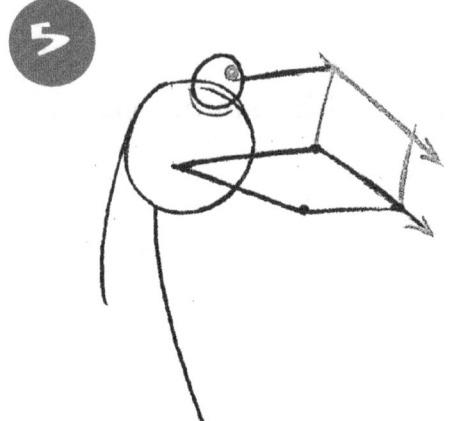

Darken in the pupils, leaving a small reflection spot. Then, add a curved **contour** line under the eye. This will give your Tearing T-rex a look of urgency as he rips all the kids' homework to shreds. Finish blocking in the upper jaw. It should look like a 3-D box.

6

When you draw the nostrils make the nostril that is closer to you larger, and the other nostril smaller and much more foreshortened. Draw the bottom of the mouth angling open like I've shown here.

ART ALERT!
Remember that near objects are always drawn larger and less foreshortened than objects that are farther away.

7

Wrinkle

Let's add a wrinkle to the edge of the snout that is closest to you. Wrinkles are just some of the bonus **details** that give our cartoon critters more character and **style**. Draw the **thickness** inside the nostril. Then, use **size** to draw the near fangs larger, and the far fangs much smaller. Add the bottom of the jaw, and block in the far arm with tapered lines. Sketch in the basic shapes for the hands and fingers.

8

Curved contour lines

Now, add one of the most important elements of our cartoon drawing lesson—the drooping, drooling tongue . . . BLAH! Overlap the tongue as it twists and droops out between the fangs and over the lower jaw. Add more detail to the overlapping fingers. Remember the fingers get smaller as they move deeper into your drawing. Sketch in the top edge of the large sheet of homework paper that T-rex is tearing to tiny tidbits.

ART ALERT!

When you draw the claws, be sure to use curved contour lines at the point where they attach to the body. If you dont, Tearing T-rex's claws will look like they were glued on with chewing gum!

9

Curved contour lines

As soon as you start to darken in the deep black nooks and crannies in your cartoon, you will see Tearing T-rex instantly pop out in 3-D. Blacken in the nostrils and the mouth. Add some details and **texture** like freckles and hair. Using spirals, draw the near edge of the ripping paper curling away from the scratching claws.

10

Wow! There is a lot of darkening of nooks and crannies to do in this cartoon—not to mention the shading and detailed texture of the scales and fingernails. Take your time with this more advanced lesson. Enjoy this final **clean up** and details process.

You are going to discover that the better you become at 3-D cartooning, the more detailed your work will become, and the longer each piece of artwork will take you to complete. Step number 10 of the Tearing T-rex lesson took me just about three hours to complete with ink and blended pencil shading. Take your time and have fun with your cartooning-in-3-D journey.

DRAW! DRAW! DRAW!

COOL CORAL COLONY

Now that we have created a new exciting world of crazy cool critters, we need to choose an environment for them to live in—like a giant forest of redwood trees, an alien planet, a cave of ice, or how about a coral reef so thick with tube coral it looks like a redwood forest underwater?!

CARTOONING LESSON #11

1

Start with two **guide dots** to create a **foreshortened** circle. The foreshortened circle will be the top of the first trunk of tube coral in your fabulous undersea forest.

2

Tapered

Taper the sides of the tube, curving the lines in just a bit to flare out the top. Begin clustering other foreshortened circle tops around the tube, using guide dots to draw the foreshortened circles. Slant these other foreshortened circles in a variety of **positions**. This will make your coral colony look really interesting, with lots of **overlapping** nooks and crannies. Taper the sides of another tube coral trunk and **block** in more tubes higher up in your picture. Make some of the foreshortened circles large and some small. Use lots of variety. Nature is the ultimate source of variety!

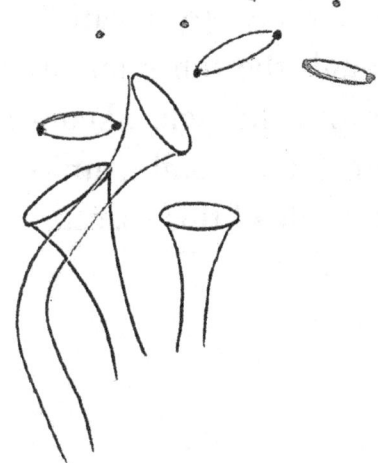

Curve a tall tube coral behind the tubes you have already drawn. Block in more foreshortened coral tube tops above them.

Go nuts with your pencil. Twist and tuck these tubes all over your page.

Clean up some of your extra lines, and overlap some more long tube coral trunks over and under one another.

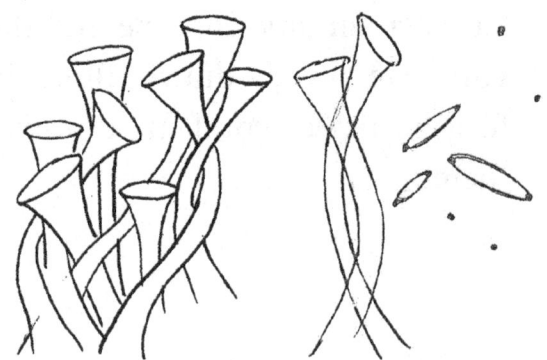

Let's leave a hole in the middle of the colony to create a tunnel through the tubes for little fishies to swim through. **Sketch** in some more tube coral trunks on the other side of this space.

Add more overlapping **details** to the tubes, and begin blocking in the fish swimming through the tunnel. You can draw a fish or any one of the crazy cartoon critters you have learned to draw in this book.

Shading

Begin darkening the **shadows** under the tubes where they overlap one another. This is a very important shadow. Add more detail to your expanding tube coral colony. Draw the pupils in the fish's eyeballs, leaving a tiny spot inside to show the reflection of the light.

ART ALERT!
When you overlap objects, shade a small dark section around the overlapped area to make the front object POP out in 3-D.

Wow! Check out the intense visual effect you can achieve when you really darken in the background! Talk about popping off your paper in 3-D! This powerful effect is called **contrast**. Drawing a really dark area next to a light area creates a visual contrast that makes the lighter areas stand out and is really pleasing to your eye. Add the sea grass swaying gently in the ocean current by drawing long S-curve lines like blades of grass. Entwine these sea grass blades in and out, around and through the weaving tube coral forest.

ART ALERT!

What a delightful environment we have created for our sea creatures to live in! Now you can modify this environment for the Drooling Dinosaurs, Bitsy Bugs, and the Meandering Mouse. These cool cartoon critters can't breathe under the sea, or can they? Perhaps draw them with scuba gear, or a giant bubble biosphere where they live in a secret city under the sea? Or maybe this isn't an underwater environment at all. Maybe it's a field of tall grass from your Bitsy Bug cartoon critter's point of view! The bugs could have an entire bugopolis city built out of these tube-shaped grass blades. Bugopolis can be complete with tube bridges, roads, and little bubble bug cars or you can start with any crazy cool cartoon critter—or two—and build a wild, fascinating, magical environment around them! YOUR own unique imagination contains millions of idea combinations for zillions of fun cartoon environments.

DRAW! DRAW! DRAW!

DRAW! DRAW! DRAW!

CONGRATULATIONS, YOUNG CARTOONING GENIUS!

You have just completed 11 very advanced 3-D cartooning lessons! I'm VERY impressed with your daily drawing diligence.

Now I want you to hang up your 3-D cartoons all over your house, your bedroom, your refrigerator! Put your brilliant masterpieces all over your classroom, your artroom, your principal's office! Display your amazing genius renderings everywhere! The world has a right to see and enjoy your amazing art!

HERE ARE A FEW POINTS TO REMEMBER...

1. Practice drawing in your cartooning journal, or sketchbook, every day. The more you practice, the more 3-D your drawings will look.

2. Create a cartoon gallery of your brilliant artwork—on your refrigerator, your bedroom door, a wall, or anywhere you can. Mail copies of your 3-D cartoons to your grandparents, aunts, uncles, and friends. I want you to share your awesome talent with your family and the whole world!

3. Be sure to visit my Web site at **WWW.MARKKISTLER.COM** to draw more cartoons and tour the digital student art gallery.

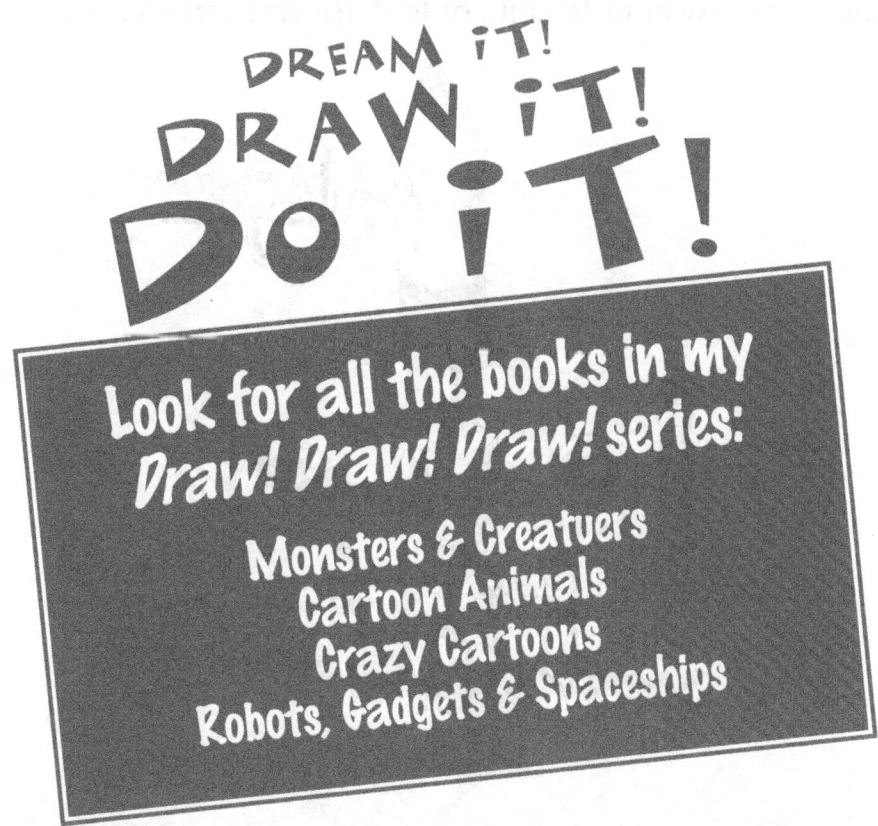

Look for all the books in my Draw! Draw! Draw! series:
- Monsters & Creatuers
- Cartoon Animals
- Crazy Cartoons
- Robots, Gadgets & Spaceships

DRAW WITH ME!

You can learn from me personally in many different ways!

- **Other books:** Find my other drawing books, for kids and for adults, in your local bookstore, in online bookstores, or on my website: www.markkistler.com.
- **Real-time classes with me:** Learn with me at school, on line, or in a summer camp!
    - **Live, weekly webcast lessons:** Interact and chat with me while you learn—I would love to see you! Sign up for my lessons at www.markkistler.com.
    - **Summer art camps:** I offer summer art camps all summer long, all over the country! Learn more at www.markkistler.com.
    - **School assemblies:** The best part of my cartooning career is having the opportunity to teach "Dare to Draw in 3-D" assemblies at more than 100 elementary schools each year. I offer both live and virtual assemblies! Visit www.markkistler.com for more information about my school visits and workshops.
- **Super awesome video lessons:** Learn at your own pace through my interactive, pre-recorded classes. I've created 400 super-cool lessons just for you. Find them at www.draw3d.com, or look for free samples on YouTube!

CARTOONING VOCABULARY WORDS

Learn these words and practice them each day in your cartooning journal. The more you practice, the more brilliantly 3-D your drawings will appear!

3-D	When you draw in "three-dimensions," you are creating a picture that has width, height, and depth. Every picture you have ever drawn has width and height. This is called a 2-D, or two-dimensional, picture. To successfully draw in 3-D you need to create the optical illusion of depth All the words below will help you create the look of depth in your picture.
Action Lines	Small curved lines drawn at the ends or tips of a cartoon to make it look like the cartoon is moving.
Alignment	Use lines you have drawn earlier in a picture as reference lines to help you know where to position new lines.
Blend	Smudge shading with your finger or a tissue to make it look like one smooth change from dark to light. Blending helps you show that an object is curved or rounded.
Blocking	Roughly draw in the basic shape of your cartoons, using light sketchy lines. This is how you begin to mold a 3-D cartoon. Then you add layers of detail, and finally clean up the extra lines.
Cartooning Journal	You really need to keep several sketchbooks or cartooning journals in different sizes on hand to draw all day long. It's easy to make a bunch of these just by gathering lots of scrap paper from your school recycling scrap paper tubs. Have your parents help you cut these stacks of papers into five different size pads of 30-50 sheets each. Make some the size of your palm, some the size of a piece of bread, some the size of a tablet, and some the size of your front door!
Cleanup	This is the final stage in creating a very cool 3-D cartoon. Use an eraser to carefully clean up any extra lines and smudges.

Contour	Lines that curve around an object to give it shape and make it look like it takes up space.
Contrast	Drawing a dark area next to a light area to make the light area stand out.
Depth	If width is how wide a cartoon is, and height is how tall a cartoon is, then depth is how much space a drawing looks like it takes up from back to front.
Details or extra bonus ideas	You really start to have fun when you begin adding lots of your own extra touches to your picture—like clothes, hair, a goofy smile, or even freckles. The more unique details you can think of to add to your cartoon, the more brilliant it will look!
Foreshortening	When you squish a shape to create the illusion that one edge is closer to you than the other.
Genius	This word describes how smart you are because you can draw 3-D cartoons so brilliantly!
Guide Dots	Always place guide dots when you are drawing foreshortened circles and foreshortened squares. These guide dots will help you keep the shapes nice and foreshortened.
Guidelines	Always use lines to lightly block in a sketch of your cartoon. Guidelines help in drawing accurate angles on cast shadows and overlapping objects, and in pushing objects way deep into your picture.
Horizon Line	Draw a line behind the objects in your picture to represent the ground. This line establishes a visual reference for your eye to relate to the ground, the sky, and the objects.
Light Source	The spot on your drawing where the light is coming from. The shadows and shading will be on the opposite side of the drawing—the side that faces away from light.
Optical Illusion	Our main goal with these cartoon drawing lessons is to trick your eye into thinking that the objects you have drawn on a flat piece of paper are popping out in 3-D!
Overlapping	To make an object in your cartoon look closer than another object, draw it in front of the other object.

Position	Draw objects lower in the picture to make them appear closer to your eye. Draw objects higher and smaller to make them appear farther away and deeper in your picture.
Professional	The word people will be using a lot to describe your remarkable cartoon illustrating skill!
Shading	Darken the side of the object that faces away from your imaginary light source. Be sure to blend this shading on curved objects, and use a solid tone on block objects. Shading is a very important key to drawing in 3-D!
Shadow	Draw shadows on the ground next to objects in your picture. Shadows should be opposite your imaginary light source to create the illusion that the object is popping off the ground and right off your paper!
Size	Draw objects larger if you want them to look closer than objects that are drawn smaller in your picture.
Sketch	The light rough lines drawn at the beginning of a drawing to get the basic shapes down on the paper. You can darken in the lines you want to keep in the final cleanup stage.
Style	You are now in the process of developing your very own unique cartooning style. This means that when you display your amazing 3-D cartoons at your school's art show, people will be able to immediately recognize which pictures you drew. Even if there are 8,000 other pictures hanging. Even if there are no names on the artwork, and even if all the pictures were colored with the same three colors! Your brilliant style stands apart from the rest.
Tapering	When part of a drawing—like Dino Dictator's chair—gets smaller and smaller at one end.
Texture	The look and feel of something—like rough, smooth, or hairy.
Thickness	Lines that help show how wide part of your gadget or gizmo is. Thickness can make canyons look deep, fish lips look blubbery, and nostrils look 3-D.

MARK KISTLER - BIOGRAPHY

Mark Kistler, with inimitable enthusiasm and style, has taught millions of children how to draw through his bestselling books, his popular PBS television series, his on and off-line classes and summer camps, and his more than seven thousand school assembly workshops around the world, including Australia, Germany, England, Scotland, Mexico, Japan, Spain and the United States.

He starred as Commander Mark and Captain Mark in the hit PBS television series The Secret City, The Draw Squad, The New Secret City Adventures, and his self-produced PBS series Mark Kistler's Imagination Station, which won an Emmy Award in 2010.

Mark's children's books include *Learn to Draw with Commander Mark, Mark Kistler's Draw Squad, The Imagination Station, Drawing in 3-D with Mark Kistler*, and the four-book series *Draw! Draw! Draw!* (originally titled *Dare to Draw in 3-D!*). His first book written for adults, *You Can Draw in 30 Days*, has become a category leader and perennial bestseller.

Online, Mark offers popular live and recorded classes. His YouTube videos alone have generated more than a million views. He has received more than a million letters and emails containing 3-D drawings from children around the world.

Mark deeply believes that learning how to draw builds a child's critical thinking skills while nourishing self-esteem. His positive messages on self-image, goal setting, dream questing, environmental awareness and the power of reading have inspired millions of children to discover their awesome individual potential.

Mark lives with his children in Houston, Texas, United States.

www.MarkKistler.com || www.MarkKistlerLive.com || www.draw3D.com
Facebook: https://www.facebook.com/artistMarkKistler
Twitter: @Mark_Kistler

Made in the USA
Monee, IL
27 December 2024